Passport to the War

Passport to the War

A SELECTION OF POEMS BY

STANLEY
KUNITZ

HENRY HOLT AND COMPANY · NEW YORK

First Printing

PRINTED IN THE UNITED STATES OF AMERICA

To Eleanor

CONTENTS

PART ONE

PART TWO

NOTE

Part II of this book contains a selection of poems, some of them revised, from an earlier volume now out of print (*Intellectual Things,* Doubleday, Doran, 1930). Part I includes all my poems written since then that I wish to keep. Neither section is arranged chronologically. Certain of the poems have appeared previously in *Poetry: A Magazine of Verse, The Nation, The New Republic, The Saturday Review of Literature, The Commonweal, Partisan Review, Direction, Hound and Horn, The Dial, The American Mercury, The New American Caravan.*

S. K.

Part One

REFLECTION BY A MAILBOX

When I stand in the center of that man's madness,
Deep in his trauma, as in the crater of a wound,
My ancestors step from my American bones.
There's mother in a woven shawl, and that,
No doubt, is father picking up his pack
For the return voyage through those dreadful years
Into the winter of the raging eye.

One generation past, two days by plane away,
My house is dispossessed, my friends dispersed,
My teeth and pride knocked in, my people game
For the hunters of man-skins in the warrens of Europe,
The impossible creatures of an hysteriac's dream
Advancing with hatchets sunk into their skulls
To rip the god out of the machines.

Are these the citizens of the new estate
To which the continental shelves aspire;
Or the powerful get of a dying age, corrupt
And passion-smeared, with fluid on their lips,
As if a soul had been given to petroleum?

How shall we uncreate that lawless energy?

Now I wait under the hemlock by the road
For the red-haired postman with the smiling hand
To bring me my passport to the war.
Familiarly his car shifts into gear
Around the curve; he coasts up to my drive; the day
Strikes noon; I think of Pavlov and his dogs
And the motto carved on the broad lintel of his brain:
"Sequence, consequence, and again consequence."

MY SURGEONS

My surgeons are a savage band,
Surely their patient is ill-fated.
Their tricks are coarse: the small sweet hand
I seized was wax, or amputated.
With the humiliated swollen-footed
And the lost persecuted their traps are baited.

Deftly they opened the brain of a child,
And it was full of flying dreams;
Father was prowling in a field
With speckled tongue and a collar of flame.
They labeled it "Polluted Streams,"
The body floating with the name.

They studied a prostrate fever-chart
With unmitigating eyes; one said,
"Bohemian germs, Weltschmerz, bad art
And Spanish fly. Off with his head."
Another, "Fascist. His boot is filled with blood."
They cut me up till I was red.

Lastly they squeezed out of my veins
The bright liquor of sympathy;
I lost the touch of souls, the reins
On white revenge, and I was free
Of pity, a solid man of snow.
But in the night to whom could I go?

Lie down with me, dear girl, before
My butcher-boys begin to rave.
"No hope for persons any more,"
They cry, "on either side of the grave."
Tell them I say the heart forgives
The world. Yes, I believe. In love.

THE TUTORED CHILD

Your mother, whom the mirror-world has claimed,
Plucks at the telltale hairs with violent hand
And thinks time backward to a brassy song,
Rolling the grape of hysteria under her tongue.

Your father, in whom two ambitions rave,
Like stations wrangling on the foreign wave
For spheres of influence, loathes the heart that blends
His guilty love; but the quarrel never ends.

You are of nature's bright unlucky brood,
Born of the drop of talent in your blood
Wherewith the gates of mystery are oiled.
Mortals will touch you and your taste be spoiled,

Witches in metals test you. I observe
Defeat, taking short cuts from nerve to nerve,
Climb through the narrow transom of your will;
And I weep, for having made you vulnerable.

My poor poor child whose terrors never cease,
Here is my pity penny. Buy you peace.

THE SIGNAL FROM THE HOUSE

I said to the watcher at the gate,
"They also kill who wait."

I cried to the mourner on the stair,
"Mother, I hate you for those tears."

To mistress of the ruined hall,
The keeper of the sacred heart,

I brought the mind's indifference
And the heavy marble of my face.

For these who were too much with me
Were secretly against me:

Hostages to the old life,
Expecting to be ransomed daily

And for the same fond reason
From the deep prison of their person,

Their lantern shining in the window
Had signaled me, like cry of conscience,

Insisting that I must be broken
Upon the wheel of the unforsaken.

FATHER AND SON

Now in the suburbs and the falling light
I followed him, and now down sandy road
Whiter than bone-dust, through the sweet
Curdle of fields, where the plums
Dropped with their load of ripeness, one by one.
Mile after mile I followed, with skimming feet,
After the secret master of my blood,
Him, steeped in the odor of ponds, whose indomitable love
Kept me in chains. Strode years; stretched into bird;
Raced through the sleeping country where I was young,
The silence unrolling before me as I came,
The night nailed like an orange to my brow.

How should I tell him my fable and the fears,
How bridge the chasm in a casual tone,
Saying, "The house, the stucco one you built,
We lost. Sister married and went from home,
And nothing comes back, it's strange, from where she goes.
I lived on a hill that had too many rooms:
Light we could make, but not enough of warmth,
And when the light failed, I climbed under the hill.
The papers are delivered every day;
I am alone and never shed a tear."

At the water's edge, where the smothering ferns lifted
Their arms, "Father!" I cried, "Return! You know
The way. I'll wipe the mudstains from your clothes;
No trace, I promise, will remain. Instruct
Your son, whirling between two wars,
In the Gemara of your gentleness,
For I would be a child to those who mourn
And brother to the foundlings of the field
And friend of innocence and all bright eyes.
O teach me how to work and keep me kind."

Among the turtles and the lilies he turned to me
The white ignorant hollow of his face.

WELCOME THE WRATH

Poor john, who joined in make of wrong
And guessed no guile, dare I complain?—
Or practice to endure the heart unstrung,
The waiting at the door too long,
Winter, wages, and self-disdain.

Endure? That is the dialect of love,
The greenhorn of the west, my late companion,
Now straggling crossfoot half-alive
Back to his country, with crazy sleeve
Flopping, like a shot pinion.

Let him endure. I'll not: not warp my vision
To square with odds; not scrape; not scamp my fiber,
Though pushed by spoilers of the nerves' precision,
Bothered by caterpillars of suspicion,
Hired by speculators in my gut and labor.

Wrath has come down from the hills to enlist
Me surely in his brindled generation,
The race of the tiger; come down at last
Has wrath to build a bonfire of my breast
With one wet match and all man's desolation.

NIGHT LETTER

The urgent letter that I try to write
Night after night to you to whom I turn,
The staunchless word, my language of the wound,
Begins to stain the page. Here in my room
With my unkenneled need, the Faustian dog
That chews my penitential bones, I hope
And do not hope, I pray and mock my prayer,
Twisting my coils, this dangling life of mine,
Now twelve years come of age, and me unpleased
With all my ways, my very littlest ones,
My part, my lines, unless you hold them dear.
Where is your ministry? I thought I heard
A piece of laughter break upon the stair
Like glass, but when I wheeled around I saw
Disorder, in a tall magician's hat,
Keeping his rabbit-madness crouched inside,
Sit at my desk and scramble all the news.
The strangest things are happening. Christ! the dead,
Pushing the membrane from their face, salute
The dead and scribble slogans on our walls;
Phantoms and phobias mobilize, thronging
The roads; and in the Bitch's streets the men
Are lying down, great crowds with fractured wills
Dumping the shapeless burden of their lives
Into the rivers where the motors flowed.

Of those that stood in my doorway, self-accused,
Besmeared with failure in the swamps of trade,
One put a gun in his examiner's hand,
Making the judgment loud; another squats
Upon the asylum floor and plays with toys,
Like the spiral of a soul balanced on a stone,
Or a new gadget for slicing off the thumb;
The rest whirl in the torment of our time.
What have we done to them that what they are
Shrinks from the touch of what they hoped to be?

"Pardon," I plead, clutching the fragile sleeve
Of my poor father's ghost returned to howl
His wrongs. I suffer the twentieth century,
The nerves of commerce wither in my arm;
Violence shakes my dreams; I am so cold,
Chilled by the persecuting wind abroad,
The oratory of the weasel's tooth,
The slaughter of the blue-eyed open towns,
And principle disgraced, and art denied.

My dear, is it too late for peace, too late
For men to gather at the wells to drink
The sweet water; too late for fellowship
And laughter at the forge; too late for us
To say, "Let us be good unto each other"?
The lamps go singly out; the valley sleeps;
I tend the last light shining on the farms
And keep for you the thought of love alive,
As scholars dungeoned in an ignorant age
Tended the embers of the Trojan fire.
Cities shall suffer siege and some shall fall,
But man's not taken. What the deep heart means,
Its message of the big, round, childish hand,
Its wonder, its simple lonely cry,
The bloodied envelope addressed to you,
Is history, that wide and mortal pang.

THE LAST PICNIC

The guests in their summer colors have fled
Through field and hedgerow. Come, let's pick
The bones and feathers of our fun
And kill the fire with a savage stick.

The figures of our country play,
The mocking dancers, in a swirl
Of laughter waved from the evening's edge,
Wrote finis to a pastoral.

Now the tongue of the military man,
Summoning the violent,
Calls the wild dogs out of their holes
And the deep Indian from his tent,

Not to be tamed, not to be stamped
Under. Earth-faced, behind this grove,
Our failures creep with soldier hearts,
Pointing their guns at what we love.

When they shall paint our sockets gray
And light us like a stinking fuse,
Remember that we once could say,
Yesterday we had a world to lose.

THE HEMORRHAGE

The people made a ring
Around the man in the park.
He was our banished king
Of blames and staunchless flows,
Exhibitor of the dark
Abominable rose;

Our chief, returned at last
From exile, with the grim
Stamina of the lost,
To show his sovereign hurt.
Wildly we dreaded him
And the strong god of his heart

Escaping, crawling down
Ditches where papers blow,
Smearing the sills of the town,
Strangling the hydra-drains
Coiled under. Stop! We know
How much a man contains.

We picnicked all that day,
Dishonored signs that nayed us,
Pulled marigolds, were gay
Before the apes, smashed glass.
Rifles could not have made us
Keep off the bloody grass;

For we were sick of crimes
Against us, and the head
Pitched on the absorbing *Times,*
And no one to accuse,
And nothing paid for, and we read,
We read that day what blotted out the news.

THE HARSH JUDGMENT

Inside, a hundred doors by which to leave;
Outside, you never can come in again.
The gesture made is woven in the sleeve,
The spiral echo sinks into the grain.
What died in me will warn me if you turn
Not to be tender-minded, though I burn,
In time so cruel, so difficult for love.

The burden of the personal, the life
By profit plowed, the tapping of our power—
You know the long rebellion and the spleen.
Last night, last year, with the tumbling of a leaf
The autumn came. Dark leaf from darker tower
Falls miles, deeper than coals, and still goes down.
Courage! That pity made our hearts unclean.

CONFIDENTIAL INSTRUCTIONS

When, on your dangerous mission gone,
You underrate our foes as dunces,
Be wary, not of sudden gun,
But of your partner at the dances;

Lest you be tamed in dead-end alleys
Where the mind's virtue drops from sight,
Loath to unlink from darling follies
Cuddled in houses of deceit;

Or cozened dearly by the bitch
Of souls, the international spy
Whirling in young men's arms, to each
Mistress, but in old carrion's pay.

THE OLD CLOTHES MAN

Have you any old clothes to sell?
The years make a stain you can't conceal,
Your fabric's eaten, you discard
That part of your life for which you cared.

You pluck a thread from your cuff: it winces
Straight to your shoulder. Ambition grieves
In trunks and bags; moth-featured, minces
From closets, beating empty sleeves.

History stagnates in your house.
I smelt the ruinous time, will buy
Your waste of talent. There's an ooze
Of souls too virulent to die

Contagious on the baffling walls.
You sit and watch the ceiling crack;
Horror sifts through and softly falls
From worlds beyond the zodiac.

You fear the unappeasable bone
That growls in your breast, and the mind's
long feather,
The heart that imitates a stone,
And lest your hands should grow together

And violence unstring your voice.
I know what hangs behind your stair,
Spoiling with conscience and disuse:
The uniform you never wear,

The fitness and the pride, so vilely
Dishonored, the smiling target mouth,
Innocence ambushed, in the sharp volley
Reeling before the huntsmen of youth.

Therefore I come to mobilize
Your poor blind wounds, as in the coat,
The form betrayed, the defeated eyes,
My brother my groom, my dear recruit.

There will be skirmishing and loot
And fires to light our marches. Let
The enemies of life beware
When these old clothes go forth to war.

CARELESS LOVE

Who have been lonely once
Are comforted by their guns.
Affectionately they speak
To the dark beauty, whose cheek
Beside their own cheek glows.
They are calmed by such repose,
Such power held in hand;
Their young bones understand
The shudder in that frame.
Without nation, without name,
They give the load of love,
And it's returned, to prove
How much the husband heart
Can hold of it: for what
This nymphomaniac enjoys
Inexhaustibly is boys.

THE SUPPER BEFORE LAST

The intellectuals at the feast,
Emaciated on their fare,
Clap hands at the fabulous new beast
Upon the massive platter borne.
Their tongues rejoice, steeped in the rare
Juices of the unicorn;
While drunk with ptomaines now, the crow
That hoarsely to the table came,
Snatches at gobbets flung below,
And smirking in his greasy frock
Clamps beak on the honeyed mortal game
Under the dreaming hip and hock.

THE DAUGHTERS OF THE HORSELEECH

The daughters of the horseleech crying "Give! Give!"
Implore the young men for the blood of martyrs.
How shall we keep the old senator alive
Unless we satisfy his thirst for cultures?

Entreat the rat, the weasel, and the fox
To forage for a toothless master;
Have mercy, boys, on the monkey in his box;
Dear Judas goat, lead out the sheep to slaughter,

For if the warlock with the gilded claws
Withers away, and of his bones are waters,
Who will transmute our foreheads into brass
And who will keep his five charming daughters?

BETWEEN THE ACTS

Fate hired me once to play a villain's part.
I did it badly, wasting valued blood;
Now when the call is given to the good,
It is that knave who answers in my heart.

THIS DAY THIS WORLD

My architects, forsaking me,
Submit designs for a bombproof mansion;
My scholars of the fourth dimension
Complain they starve to death in three;
My correspondents write all day
The business of the enemy.

Tapped of their useful energies,
My soldiers pace the mind's frontier;
Engine recoils from engineer
And strikes at the courage in his eyes.
When shall my swarthy workmen rise,
Demand the power and the keys?

THE ILLUSIONIST

My name is sand: I make
Dumbshows on windowshades;
Wring hands; dissolve; swirl back;
Play furious, grim charades.
In airless room confined,
Thick with the curds of night,
I live upon my mind,
Am six-foot parasite;
Am envy, like a vein
Run dry; am hypocrite,
Whose bonecase (melted down)
Shimmers with scaly wit.
What have I not permitted?
What flagrant postures taken?
Nor shown the head matted
Nor the white forehead broken,
But parodied my life,
Assumed eccentric forms,
Retreated into leaf,
Made branches of my arms;
Groveled; ah, clung in hiding
To my father's rotten wall.

Kneel, spirit. At this beheading
Thy spongy faces fall.

INVOCATION

Soul of my soul, in the ancestral wood
Where all the trees were loosened of their leaves
I strayed, uncovering my winter form;

Webbed in a dream, stagnating like a worm,
Offensive to myself, to the gray bird-drifts
Melting from the boughs with rhyming calls;

Ancient and hoarse, beslimed, glued to a rock
Five hundred years, fainting, struggling with mist
Self-woven, issue of death, ghost of my name—

Heard then the pods clack hollow blistered skins
Where shaggy nest, where musty honeycomb,
Tipped in the blowing summer of your fame,

And sleazy men in cabins underground
Rose up and sang. Gleam of their eyes! by day
Harsh solar gold, and night's bleached lunar stone.

I too have known attrition in the rains,
Endured the conjugations of the stars,
Yet, Circler, one incendiary vein

I have defended, purified, to slake
You in the burning, whose daemonic beak
The clasp of bone about my heart O break!

NO WORD

Through portal and through peristyle
Her phantom glides, whose secret mouth,
The absence of whose flagrant smile,
Hangs on my chimney like a wreath of cloud.

I prod the coals; my tortured faith
Kneels in the blaze on melting paws;
Jeweled with tears, the lonely beast
Bequeaths me irony and claws.

No message. May the mothering dark,
Whose benediction calms the sea,
Abater of the atrocious spark
Of love and love's anxiety,

Be kind; and may my self condone,
As surely as my judge reprieves,
This heart strung on the telephone,
Folded in death, whom no voice revives.

THE LAST QUESTION

Oh the good times! the laughter on the hill!
The parties down at Larry's in the spring!
Your sovereign pleasure, careless itself to save,
Goes naked at the heart. Touching, you bring
Rumors of heaven and its generous spoils
Here, even, where our hooded shadows rise
To play the stab-scene, the end of love,
While grief intones, ever the third that stays.
Now that your pity shines in other hall,
Now that your grain again comes to the mill,
Shall I be happy soon, shall I rejoice,
Or wrestle with that stranger whom you praise?

HOW LONG IS THE NIGHT?

On the anvil of love my flesh has been hammered out.
Indifferent, in the indifferent air,
I circulate and suck the star-space in.
No one is dear to me now,
Leastly myself that sickened in the night.
I would abandon this loose bag of bones
And walk between the world's great wounds, unpitying.

THE GUILTY MAN

The years of my life were odd that now are even.
Think! to be young, amused, and not a fool;
Playing the world's game—think!—with world's own rules,
And nothing lost, I think, I think . . . but years.
Heart against mouth is singing out of tune,
Night's whisperings and blanks betrayed; this is
The end of lies: my bones are angry with me.

Father, the darkness of the self goes out
And spreads contagion on the flowing air.
I walk obscurely in a cloud of dark:
Yea, when I kneeled, the dark kneeled down with me.
Touch me: my folds and my defenses fall;
I stand within myself, myself my shield.

Teach me my reasons, I would know their names,
Cry scandal, drive my secrets out, because
I hate the good-enough that spoils the world.
Depart from me, therefore, you virtuous men
Whose treason is to turn the conscience kind.
None may forgive us for the ancient wrongs.

THE FITTING OF THE MASK

"Again I come to buy the image fated."
"Your valued image, sir, and that's a pity,
Is gone, I mean the youth, the undefeated,
Whose falcon-heart, winged with the golden shout
Of morning, sweeps windward from his native city,
Crying his father's grief, his mother's doubt."

"You knew I cared, and that I'd come for him;
The traffic hindered me; you should have known."
"Ah there, that's bad! But my poor memory's dim
As a bell that rings the tide in; I lose track
Of things to keep and things to sell, and one
Can never be quite certain who'll come back."

"Enough! There was another face, a bright
Pathetic one I'll take, from whose wild stain
Of sympathy a man could borrow light."
"Our catalogue describes him 'Fool of Love,
Fragile and dear, tinctured with mortal pain,
Buys grain of his grain and eats the chaff thereof.' "

"Your cataloguer has the cynic touch,
But I'll forgive him. Is our business over?"
"Be patient, sir. You would not thank me much
Or recommend my baffling merchandise
If I should offer this unblessed believer,
This torn-cheek, with the chasm in his eyes."

"Old man, I'm in a hurry to proceed,
And everyone, you know, must wear a mask.
Give me a countenance to meet my need
Or malice will expose me at the dance."
"Oh sir, we'll try, but it's no easy task
To make adjustments to your circumstance;

And now, while my assistant turns the key
And in the windows now the lights go out,
For it is closing time irrevocably
Until new features sit upon the forms,
I'll sing a little ditty to the ghost
That occupies this world of empty frames.

Sings:

Good-fellow's lost among our Psychic Cases,
The Angry Man has turned a ghastly blue,
Munich exhausted all our Judas-faces,
And what are we to do, and what to do?
The Optimist was mangled in a sock,
The rats conferred and ate The Wandering Jew,
There's nothing left that's decent in our stock,
And what are we to do, and what to do?

But look!—here's something rare, macabre, a true
Invention of the time's insomniac wits.
Perhaps we ought to sell it to the zoo.
Go to the darkening glass that traps your shames
And tell me what you see."
"O Prince of Counterfeits,
This is the Self I hunted and knifed in dreams!"

OPEN THE GATES

Within the city of the burning cloud,
Dragging my life behind me in a sack,
Naked I prowl, scourged by the black
Temptation of the blood grown proud.

Here at the monumental door,
Carved with the curious legend of my youth,
I brandish the great bone of my death,
Beat once therewith and beat no more.

The hinges groan: a rush of forms
Shivers my name, wrenched out of me.
I stand on the terrible threshold, and I see
The end and the beginning in each other's arms.

"WHAT HAVE YOU DONE?"

Pigeon, who are to me
Language and light
And the long flight home,
Your question comes with coils
Like years behind,
Which I am crawling from.
Be patient with my wound:
Too long I lay
In the folds of my preparation,
Sinuous in the sun,
A golden skin,
All pride, sores, excretion,
Blazing with death. O child,
From my angry side
Tumbles this agate heart,
Your prize, veined with the root
Of guilty life,
From which flow love and art.

Part Two

CHANGE

Dissolving in the chemic vat
Of time, man (gristle and fat),
Corrupting on a rock in space
That crumbles, lifts his impermanent face
To watch the stars, his brain locked tight
Against the tall revolving night.
Yet is he neither here nor there
Because the mind moves everywhere;
And he is neither now nor then
Because tomorrow comes again
Foreshadowed, and the ragged wing
Of yesterday's remembering
Cuts sharply the immediate moon;
Nor is he always: late and soon
Becoming, never being, till
Becoming is a being still.

Here, Now, and Always, man would be
Inviolate eternally:
This is his spirit's trinity.

GEOMETRY OF MOODS

Concentrical, the universe and I
Rotated on God's crystal axletree,

So perfectly adjusted in suspense
I could not mark our split circumference,

But sphere in sphere, devotion in devotion,
Was a thing of folding air, a windy motion.

My spinal pole, tipped with a globe of light,
Stretched long as time into the infinite,

And when I turned to look upon the face
Of love's incarnate form, tremendous space

Inclined upon her mouth, the natural nest
Where, throbbing like a bird, singed thought might rest.

Concentrical, the universe and I
Rotated on God's crystal axletree,

I core of the world, a bead in a ball of glass
So pure that only Nothing could be less.

Oh the earth ensphered me, liberal and warm,
When the curve of heaven was her sleeping arm.

Now cubical upon a fractured pole
It creaks, scraping the circle of my soul.

FOR THE WORD IS FLESH

O ruined father dead, long sweetly rotten
Under the dial, the time-dissolving urn,
Beware a second perishing, forgotten,
Heap fallen leaves of memory to burn
On the slippery rock, the black eroding heart,
Before the wedged frost splits it clean apart.

The nude hand drops no sacramental flower
Of blood among the tough upthrusting weeds.
Senior, in this commemorative hour,
What shall the quick commemorate, what deeds
Ephemeral, what dazzling words that flare
Like rockets from the mouth to burst in air?

Of hypochondriacs that gnawed their seasons
In search of proofs, Lessius found twenty-two
Fine arguments, Tolet gave sixty reasons
Why souls survive. And what are they to you?
And, father, what to me, who cannot blur
The mirrored brain with fantasies of Er,

Remembering such factual spikes as pierce
The supplicating palms, and by the sea
Remembering the eyes, I hear the fierce
Wild cry of Jesus on the holy tree,
Yet have of you no syllable to keep,
Only the deep rock crumbling in the deep.

Observe the wisdom of the Florentine
Who, feeling death upon him, scribbled fast
To make revision of a deathbed scene,
Gloating that he was accurate at last.
Let sons learn from their lipless fathers how
Man enters hell without a golden bough.

TWILIGHT

I wait. I deepen in the room.
Fed lions, glowing, congregate
In corners, sleep and fade. For whom
It may concern I, tawny, wait.

Time flowing through the window; day
Spilling on the board its bright
Last blood. Folding (big, gauzy, gray),
A moth sits on the western light.

Sits on my heart that, darkened, drips
No honey from its punctured core,
Yet feeds my hands and feeds my lips.
The Moon, the Moon, is at the door!

SINGLE VISION

Before I am completely shriven
I shall reject my inch of heaven,

Cancel my eyes, and, standing, sink
Into my deepest self; there drink

Memory down. The banner of
My blood, unfurled, will not be love,

Only the pity and the pride
Of it, pinned to my open side.

When I have utterly refined
The composition of my mind,

Shaped language of my marrow till
Its forms are instant to my will,

Suffered the leaf of my heart to fall
Under the wind, and, stripping all

The tender blanket from my bone,
Rise like a skeleton in the sun,

I shall have risen to disown
The good mortality I won.

Directly risen with the stain
Of life upon my crested brain,

Which I shall shake against my ghost
To frighten him, when I am lost.

Gladly, as any poison, yield
My halved conscience, brightly peeled;

Infect him, since we live but once,
With the unused evil in my bones.

I'll shed the tear of souls, the true
Sweat, Blake's intellectual dew,

Before I am resigned to slip
A dusty finger on my lip.

PROMISE ME

Only, when I am sudden loss
Of consequence for mind and stair,
Picking my dogged way from us
To whom, recessive in some where
Of recollection, with the cross
Fallen, the breast in disrepair:

Only, when loosening clothes, you lean
Out of your window sleepily,
And with luxurious, lidded mien
Sniff at the bitter dark—dear she,
Think somewhat gently of, between
Love ended and beginning, me.

POEM

O Heart: this is a dream I had, or not a dream.
Lovingly, lovingly, I wept, but my tears did not rhyme.

In the year of my mother's blood, when I was born,
She buried my innocent head in a field, because the earth

Was sleepy with the winter. And I spoke the corn,
And I cried the clover up, with the dewy mouth of my mirth.

In the honey of summer my brain conceived: a child, I flowered
Over the maiden-stalks, drinking sweet upper light,

For I was intimate with the sun, till he devoured
Me utterly, O Heart, his tenderest neophyte.

So I died. Small gluttonous birds picked on my limpid brow,
My pale drooped feet were manacled with rushing worms;

And when I was sufficiently dead (Torturer Thou!)
I was born again. Dissolving, memory reforms

The cyclic hour I pulled life's bony root, slow inch
By inch, from its loamy trap; shrilly, like a mandrake, screamed

To rip the cord, suck liberal air, after the pinch
Of planetary rock. Womanly, a shadow combed

Her dark tremendous hair beyond the violet border
Of my sleep. Strong passionate hands I had, but could not find

The red position of her heart, nor the subtle order
Of her lips and breasts, nor the breathing cities of her mind.

Lovingly, lovingly, I wept for her absent eyes,
Large pity of her thought; I broke the spine of my pride

Upon a stone, seeing she did not recognize
My tears, because our sorrows did not coincide.

Softly grieving, ironic with a smile forlorn,
I took my baffled head and buried it under the corn.

O Heart: this is a dream I had, or not a dream.

DECIDUOUS BRANCH

Winter, that coils in the thickets now,
Will glide from the fields; the swinging rain
Be knotted with flowers; on every bough
A bird will meditate again.

Lord, in the night if I should die,
Who entertained your thrilling worm,
Corruption wastes more than the eye
Can pick from this imperfect form.

I lie awake, hearing the drip
Upon my sill; thinking, the sun
Has not been promised; we may strip
Passion to seed, and be undone.

Bleed, as the antler of the eaves
Vanishes, drop by drop. I brood
On a Christian thing: unless the leaves
Perish, the tree is not renewed.

If all our perishable stuff
Be nourished to its rot, we clean
Our trunk of death, and in our tough
And final growth are evergreen.

THE WORDS OF THE PREACHER

Taking infection from the vulgar air
And sick with the extravagant disease
Of life, my soul rejected the sweet snare
Of happiness; declined
That democratic bait, set in the world
By fortune's old and mediocre mind.

To love a changing shape with perfect faith
Is waste of faith; to follow dying things
With deathless hope is vain; to go from breath
To breath, so to be fed
And put to sleep, is cheat and shame—because
By piecemeal living a man is doomed, I said.

For time with clever fingers ties the knot
Of life that is extended like a rope,
And bundling up the spinning of our thought
(The ribbons and the lace
That might have made a garment for the wind),
Constricts our substance to a cipher's space.

Into the middle of my thought I crept
And on the bosom of the angel lay,
Lived all my life at once; and oh I wept
My own future to be;
Upon his death-soft burning plumage wept
To vie with God for His eternity.

AMBERGRIS

This body, tapped of every drop of breath,
In vast corruption of its swollen pride,
Is perfected to be the whale of death;
Yet, I believe, the hand that plumbs its side
Will gather dissolution's sweet increase,
Exquisite fern of death–in nature, ambergris.

Meanwhile, thinking of love, I have been dressed
For such destruction. Though it surely break,
Come pluck the deep wild kernel of my breast,
That wafer of devotion, and partake
Of its compacted sweetness, till it bring
The soul to rise upon the fleshly wing.

If gentle hearts are scorned, in scorn of it
I shall immerse it in such bitterness,
Bathe every pulse in such an acid wit,
That from my mammoth, cold, and featureless
Event of age, my enemies will flee,
Whereas my friends will stay and pillage me.

APPROACH OF AUTUMN

The early violets we saw together,
Lifting their delicate swift heads
As if to dip them in the water, now wither.
Arching no more like thoroughbreds.

Slender and pale, they flee the rime
Of death: the ghosts of violets
Are running in a dream. Heart-flowering time
Decays, green goes, and the eye forgets.

Forgets? But what spring-blooded stock
Sprouts deathless violets in the skull
That, pawing on the hard and bitter rock
Of reason, make thinking beautiful?

SOUL'S ADVENTURE

I heard the centuries tick slowly,
Earth's pulse equivocate. O Lord,
Gigantic silence strikes: Thy holy
And undeniable Word.

This is the bitter promised day
When, dragging wings, I leave behind
A faunlike head upon a tray,
Spear buried in the mind.

Now I must tread the starry wrack
And penetrate the burning sea.
Dear mortal boy, I may come back,
But do not wait for me.

HE

He runs before the wise men: He
Is moving on the hills like snow.
No gifts, no tears, no company
He brings, but wind-rise and water-flow.

In meadows of descended day
His motion leans, dividing air:
He takes the unforgiving way
Beneath the apostolic star.

Mary, Mary, call Him stranger.
Parting the night's long hair, He steals
Within the heart, that humble manger
Where the white, astonished spirit kneels.

His vertical inflicting pride,
Whose shadow cuts the nib of space,
Bends to this virtue fructified.
But though He kiss the little face

Like rapture breaking on the mind,
The necessary fierce details
Implacably He has designed.
Redemption hangs upon the nails.

PROPHECY ON LETHE

Echo, the beating of the tide,
Infringes on the blond curved shore;
Archaic weeds from sleep's green side
Bind skull and pelvis till the four
Seasons of the blood are unified.

Anonymous sweet carrion,
Blind mammal floating on the stream
Of depthless sound, completely one
In the cinnamon-dark of no dream—
A pod of silence, bursting when the sun

Clings to the forehead, will surprise
The gasping turtle and the leech
With your strange brain blooming as it lies
Abandoned to the bipeds on the beach;
Your jelly-mouth and, crushed, your polyp eyes.

LOVERS RELENTLESSLY

Lovers relentlessly contend to be
Superior in their identity:

The compass of the ego is designed
To circumscribe intact a lesser mind

With definition; tender thought would wrest
Each clean protective secret from the breast;

Affection's eyes go deep, make morbid lesion
In pride's tissue, are ferocious with possession;

Love's active hands insistently caress
The quivering body of shy loveliness,

Hands that are desperately moved to own
The subtly reasoned flesh on branching bone;

Lovers regard the simple moon that spills
White magic in a garden, bend their wills

Obliquely on each other; lovers eat
The small ecstatic heart to be complete;

Engaged in complicate analysis
Of passionate destruction, lovers kiss;

In furious involvement they would make
A double meaning single. Some must break

Upon the wheel of love, but not the strange,
The secret lords, whom only death can change.

FOR PROSERPINE

Our purple tongues that testify
The pomegranate has been broken
Are stained, their roots and buds are stained, with the shy
Fruity pleasure of us, met, spoken.

(I shall remember the days
Of my youth and your beautiful new ways.)

In fierce decay I'll find a stripe
Of honey sweetening the tart
Old brain. I shall not know again such ripe
Beauty of the burst, dark heart.

(I'll think of my absurd,
Impossible, pledged, serious word.)

My undivulged interior world
A country for our souls shall be,
Till I am done with name and number, gnarled
And mindless like a babbling tree.

(A heavy bird will brood
On women stagnant in their blood.)

Preserve you from the long farewell
Whose sex is flowers, whose breasts are grain.
Return, return. Into a leafless hell
Gradually drops the brain.

(The bulls, the stallions, have tasted
Incredible fruit. Their seed is wasted.)

I DREAMED THAT I WAS OLD

I dreamed that I was old: in stale declension
Fallen from my prime, when company
Was mine, cat-nimbleness, and green invention,
Before time took my leafy hours away.

My wisdom, ripe with body's ruin, found
Itself tart recompense for what was lost
In false exchange: since wisdom in the ground
Has no apocalypse or pentecost.

I wept for my youth, sweet passionate young thought,
And cozy women dead that by my side
Once lay: I wept with bitter longing, not
Remembering how in my youth I cried.

NIGHT-PIECE

And everywhere, all over, men have sighed
Good night, remembering of women the bright
Of eyes; put out their bodies like a light,
And set their brains adrift upon their blood.

Let us be shy again like feathered things,
Stroll in the gardens of the spectrum (all
Last summer). Waiting for the first snowfall,
Hear colors dropping, and the dark flurry of wings.

Prevent that deepmost dream. Think late, think soon,
Of crickets, Marvell, roses, and the bare
Shoulders of teasing Venus, and O the hair
Tumbling all over, everywhere, the moon.

Up ever so many stairs it is a new
Sweet (look! it's) morning in each other's arms.
Tell me, yes I truly, by what charms
Have I been, darling, yes I really do.

I think that it is so: but did I scream
Out of my middle sleep, believe I saw
The great fish tunneling the purple sea,
Earth-darkening bird suspended over dream.

LAST WORDS

Listen: from sleep's long pillow I arise
To go away. One moment let me lean
On falling air before I lock my eyes.
Are the leaves red now? No matter. Trees are green.

The colors of the world are permanent
Despite the bleach of change. Pure stain on stain,
The bow of light's eternal forms is bent
Across steep heaven in the general brain.

Who cries, The beautiful, the proud, are fallen!
(O silly child, it was myself that cried.)
Death, eater of the heads of flowers, spills pollen:
Our little strength, our beauty, and our pride

Are for the race to keep; we can discover
Secrets with our broken skulls; our dead feet run
Under the lid of earth that closes over
The generations marching to the sun.

SO INTRICATELY IS THIS WORLD RESOLVED

So intricately is this world resolved
Of substance arched on thrust of circumstance,
The earth's organic meaning so involved
That none may break the pattern of his dance;
Lest, deviating, he confound the line
Of reason with the destiny of race,
And, altering the perilous design,
Bring ruin like a rain on time and space.

Lover, it is good to lie in the sweet grass
With a dove-soft nimble girl. But O lover,
Lift no destroying hand; let fortune pass
Unchallenged, beauty sleep; dare not to cover
Her mouth with kisses by the garden wall,
Lest, cracking in bright air, a planet fall.

ORGANIC BLOOM

The brain constructs its systems to enclose
The steady paradox of thought and sense;
Momentously its tissued meaning grows
To solve and integrate experience.
But life escapes closed reason. We explain
Our chaos into cosmos, cell by cell,
Only to learn of some insidious pain
Beyond the limits of our charted hell,
A guilt not mentioned in our prayers, a sin
Conceived against the self. So, vast and vaster
The plasmic circles of gray discipline
Spread outward to include each new disaster.
Enormous floats the brain's organic bloom
Till, bursting like a fruit, it scatters doom.

IN A STRANGE HOUSE

The memory of time is here imprisoned
In these walls, not fluent time that moves
Upon the flood, but time already reasoned
And undone of its quick eyes and loves.

We who are strangers in this finished house
Have slept with tossing shadows, and we lie
Astonished in our chambers lest we rouse
The strong assassins with a cry.

The dead would murder action. Oh, I know
Their subtle ways. They separate with fear
The fiery lips of thought. And I shall go
By silent lanes and leave you timeless here.

BEYOND REASON

The blessing in this conscious fruit, the hurt
Which is unanswerable, fill the brow
With early death. O Sion of my heart,
The milk of love were charitable now.

I do not come intent to be your lord,
Nor to contract the empire of your flight,
But as the long eye holds the spinning bird
Enclosed in the circumference of sight

And yet the bird is infinitely free
To dip its beak into the thinnest air,
So do I stand. I am not destiny
To color time or plot a hemisphere.

Creatures that carry in their little blood
Malignant influences moved to keep
Delight from love, the lonely from the proud,
Destroy themselves to live. If in my sleep

The ape, the serpent, and the fox I find
Shut with my soul in fortune's writhing sack,
I tame them with the sections of my mind
And teach my mind to love its thoughtless crack.

VITA NUOVA

I abdicate my daily self that bled,
As others breathe, for porridge it might sup.
Henceforth apocalypse will get my bread
For me. I bit my tongue and gnawed my lip,
But now the visor of my name is up.

Giving to love my undivided nature,
Cherishing life, the only fire to keep,
I have been otherwise a part-time creature,
With many selves to fool myself with hope,
And in myself a gentler self to weep.

Now I will peel that vision from my brain
Of numbers wrangling in a common place,
And I will go, unburdened, on the quiet lane
Of my eternal kind, till shadowless
With inner light I wear my father's face.

Moon of the soul, accompany me now,
Shine on the colosseums of my sense,
Be in the tabernacles of my brow.
My dark will make, reflecting from your stones,
The single beam of all my life intense.